Can it be about me?

Poems by

CHERYL MOSKOWITZ

Illustrated by

ROS ASQUITH

Contents

When I decided to write poems about being at primary school, I thought I'd better remind myself what it's like. It has been quite a long time since I was there.

I asked at the local school if I could come in and be a 'fly on the wall' to gather some ideas.

Being a fly on the wall means you sit and observe what is going on without being noticed. But I am not a fly and wasn't exactly invisible.

One boy, John, was particularly keen to know what I was doing there. He was a very smiley boy who was known for only ever wearing shorts, even when it was snowing.

John asked me why I was sitting in the corner making notes. I told him that I was trying to get ideas for some poems. He suggested that the first poem be about him.

Can it be about me?

Are you writing a poem
will it be long
can it be about me?
My name is John.
I don't have any
trousers on.
I just wear shorts
for all the year
but don't write that
because it doesn't rhyme.

In one class everyone liked to speak out. But they were supposed to put their hands up before they did. It sometimes took a long time for Miss Chapman, the teacher, to call on everyone.

It can be frustrating to wait, especially if you have something really important you want to tell people.

One little girl had her hand up for a long time, trying to do everything right so she would be picked. I think I know how she felt.

Martha wants to say something

Oh Miss, I have a good one
please look over here at me
I've been sitting still as anything
surely you can see.

I'm not fidgeting like William
or kicking Ahmed's chair
I've been waiting very patiently
so it really isn't fair.

I've got my finger on my lips
and my arm raised overhead
Once you almost saw it
but you chose Eleanor instead.

I'm not shouting out like Isobel
or pulling Holly's hair
I'm minding my own business
so it really isn't fair.

I've planned exactly how to say it
this thing I want to say
I'm crossing all my fingers
so that you will look this way.

I'm not daydreaming like Thomas
or giggling like Keir
I'm being good as gold
so Miss, it really isn't fair.

There's only five more minutes
until the home bell goes
I'm keeping all my fingers crossed
and now I've crossed my toes.

I didn't burp out loud like Roxy
she said she did it for a dare
I wouldn't be so silly, Miss
so you see it really isn't fair.

Three minutes now, oh thank you, Miss
you really aren't so rotten
You've asked me what I want to say
but . . . now I have forgotten!

There are two sides (at least) to every argument.

Some schools have a uniform, some don't. This one didn't. But that didn't stop some people thinking that it should.

I never had to wear a uniform when I was at primary school, but sometimes I wished that I could.

Reasons

Reasons to wear a uniform:

so I don't have to think too hard when I get dressed
    in the morning
so me and my friend can be twins
because my mum thinks I should

Reasons to wear whatever I want:

so I can look at the day and decide what's right to put on
so my friends can't copy me
because my mum thinks I shouldn't

On some mornings, even before you open your eyes to see what the day looks like outside, you know you'd rather spend it in bed.

That's just how it is.

Some days you're just not meant to go out

It is a dog barking, nose dripping, pavement tripping,
finger flicking, boy spitting
kind of day.
If I had my way
I'd rather stay in
then I could say
it's a TV watching, teddy hugging, toast eating,
book reading, bed snuggling,
curtain closed
kind of day
and so much better
that way.

In this school the Infants and the Juniors share the same building.

To the Juniors, the Infants can seem quite babyish and to the Infants the Juniors look big.

Being a Junior isn't always easy but it is nice being looked up to by the Infants.

Lunchbox hero

I saw her crying in the corridor
on my way back from the loo.
I recognised her from the playground,
the little blonde girl from Year 2.

They were really runny tears,
snot was dripping from her nose.
"I think I've lost something," she snivelled.
I said, "That's how it goes."

That didn't seem to help her much,
she just kept right on bawling.
I felt really stupid standing there
while all my friends were calling.

"What's the matter, then?" I whispered
so that no one else would hear.
She looked up at me and smiled
and sort of wiped away a tear.

"Look," I said, "I'm kind of busy,
you know, I'm from Year 3?"
She said, "I've lost my lunchbox,
would you look for it with me?"

You see, I have this reputation
cos I'm in the Juniors now,
I don't really hang with Infants
but this girl needed me somehow.

"Yeah, OK," I said, "I'll help you
but I'm gonna have to make it snappy."
She smiled even bigger then
and started to look happy.

"It's pink," she said, "my lunchbox,
with Barbie on the front."
Just my luck, I thought,
as I started on the hunt.

I found it in the playground,
there was no one else who saw me.
She was so grateful for my finding it
she let me have her Peperami.

And later, after school,
when I thought all this was at an end
I saw her talking with her mum.
She said, "That's him, that's my new friend."

My heart sank for just a moment
until I thought about it some.
Why shouldn't she be proud, I thought,
and want to tell her mum?

After all, she's still an Infant
and I am in Year 3.
I'd feel just as big, if I were her
and that little girl were me.

There are lots of ways that people from the same country, or the same school, can be different from each other. Even from the same home!

In our family, three people eat meat and two of us don't.

Vegetarian

My friend is vegetarian
I'm English
we still understand each other

It's hard to stand by and watch when someone else, not you, gets all the attention.

Being jealous can make you grumpy or sad or both. It would be good if we could stop ourselves from ever feeling jealous but I'm not sure we can.

My mum used to tell me that when someone's being horrible to you it is often because they are jealous. She said you have to imagine you have a special armour around you for protection.

It's good when it works.

Jealousproof

I can't stand it when my mum
comes in to help
and is really nice to all my friends.
I sometimes think
she probably likes them more than me –

But I think I might be jealousproof
in fact, I know I am.

It makes me mad
when people show off
all the new things they have got
and bring them into school
and pass them around for us to see –

Still, I think I might be jealousproof
in fact, I know I am.

I hate it when a new girl comes
and is so popular that
everyone wants to play with her
and crowds around
wanting to be her friend –

But I think I might be jealousproof
in fact, I know I am

It's annoying in assembly
when someone from the other class
gets a special prize
and the Head tells us to clap
while they go up to shake her hand –

Still I think I might be jealousproof
in fact, I know I am.

But there's really no accounting for
the way people say they like you
and then they push you away
and call you names
and won't sit next to you at lunch –

I have a hunch...

that they're not jealousproof
at least, not the way I am!

The playground can be tiring. Just standing and watching everyone else run around can make me tired.

Not everyone gets tired when they play, but it seems to me that there ought to be a way to refuel out there when you need to, so you can carry on afterwards.

There's a boy whose dad has a racing car – he gave me this idea.

Kidstop

My dad watches motor racing, all the time.

Whenever the cars need something
like new tyres or more fuel,
they do a pit stop and loads of people rush in
and start sorting them out.

I wish they had that for kids on our playground.

I think my tank might be running a bit low.

I've always found numbers more difficult than words. I liked learning Maths at school but it seemed like just when I got the hang of what we were doing, something new to learn would come and get in the way.

In America, where I went to primary school, sums in Maths were called 'problems' and that's certainly what they felt like.

The children in Classes 3SC and 3KB spent an hour each day working on their numbers. The teacher made it fun and used words and stories to teach it but that still didn't stop me and others in the class worrying about some of it.

Number troubles

Nine sweets between four,
Two each, spread evenly
But what about the extra one?
Someone will have three!

Three halves and seven eighths
I think it would make ten
But if we're meant to write a fraction
I would have to think again

Put forty-nine in groups of seven
Why would you want to do it?
When a number's big, just leave it
There's no point in going through it

I'm getting slightly worried
By this whole division lark
This splitting into smaller groups
Leaves me in the dark

Until now I thought we'd learnt
That adding up was good
Increase your numbers like your friends
That's what I understood

Subtraction, well, it can't be helped
When numbers misbehave
You simply have to take them out
They really can't be saved

But dividing, that's another thing
It really breaks my heart
To see a number split in bits
It's tearing me apart

They say breaking up is hard to do
Not only that, it's cruel
And now we have to watch it happen
Every day at school

And now it seems that there will be
More problems on the way
Our teacher said we're going to start
On decimals today!

A cinquain is a poem of five lines. It starts with a short line of only two syllables. Then the lines get longer, increasing to 4, 6, then 8 syllables. Finally the last line is two syllables again.

The five lines tell about a single subject, what it looks like, feels like and what it does. Cinquains can be written about anything.

Sun cinquain

Sometimes
when the hot sun
burns my skin it feels like
a razor scratch rather than a
soft kiss.

Haiku is a Japanese form of poetry.
It's very short, only three lines long.
   The first and last line have five syllables.
Count them. The middle line has seven.
The whole thing makes a picture.

Haiku for summer

We are all waiting
For school to be out again
Take uniforms off

Getting a word right isn't just about the right spelling.

Some words work no matter how you write them.

T-r-e-a-s-u-r-e

Who knows how to write Treasure?

I know, Miss,
do you write it like the penny I found on my
    way to school this morning?
It wasn't that new or shiny but I picked it up
    and I made a wish...
No, I know, Miss,
do you write it like my baby sister? (My
    mum says she is one)

For ages I thought she was really stupid and
    boring but yesterday at dinner I put a
    carrot up my nose and she laughed.
No one else did, but she did...
Miss, do you write it like the stuff you keep
    in a box that's private and no one else can
    look at?

I have one of those and I've got my hair in it,
   the first bit of hair that got cut off only I
   didn't tie it together or anything so it came
   apart and got over all the other things like
   the necklace my Grandma gave me and
   my Lego Club badge...
Miss, I know, I know –

do you write it like when the sun has almost
   disappeared but not quite and there's this
   massive pink glow that looks like bubble
   gum spread all over the sky only it's not
   sticky but kind of shiny like a pearl...?
Miss, is it a ladybird with a million trillion
   spots on it so it can live forever...?
Or Miss, Miss,
is it like my La-La I've had it since I was
   small, it's really a little duvet, like a
   cover, but I call it my La-La and I take it
   everywhere except for school...?
Miss, is it bells ringing, Miss,
like angels singing or from a church when
   they go on and on for ages and you end
   up thinking they've come right inside
   your head to stay there singing like that
   forever...?

Miss, I know, I know, do you write it like
    it's locked in a trunk...?
Yeah, Miss, or buried in the ground...
Or, Miss,
could it be lost at the bottom of the sea, or
    hidden in a pirate's ship that's sunk or
    something...?
Miss, that's just stupid, Miss, there's no
    such thing as pirates...
There is, Miss,
but I know, Miss, can I have a go, Miss?
Do you write it like this, Miss...
T-R-E-J-A
...am I right, Miss, am I right?

Well... yes, you all were, nearly.

It's good to keep pencil and paper
with you wherever you go.
   That way if you think of something
you can write it down – it might just
turn out to be a little poem.

Moments of thought

If it's true that friends
should stick together like glue
why do they break up?

                    I can't find my heart
                    it was beating really fast
                    then it disappeared

Whispers don't only
carry secrets, they sometimes
bring surprises too

                    My lunchbox looks like
                    hers but inside you can tell
                    different mums made them

When a sum is hard
it needs a good combing through
just like tangled hair

                    There is nothing like
                    the first time you tie your shoes
                    without any help

Learning about history can be confusing.
Especially ancient history.

The things you learn about are sometimes even older than your teacher, or your mum.

On learning about Egypt in Class 3SC

Why is Miss Chapman talking
about Mummy in this place?
Mummy is at home and
she hasn't got a painted face.

She doesn't live inside a pyramid
or surround herself with gold
and though she's getting on a bit
Mum's not thousands of years old!

She was never friends with pharaohs
she doesn't even know the Queen
and as far as I know, Egypt's
somewhere that Mummy's never been.

Miss Chapman said that Mummies
are a very treasured find
I told Mummy what she told us
Mum said, "Your teacher's very kind!"

When they were learning about Egypt, Year 3 got to dress up as pharaohs and mummies. They even got to lie in a real sarcophagus. They made masks and painted them to look like Egyptian gods and goddesses.

And they made 'bastets'. Bastet was a goddess who protected the ancient Egyptian people and brought joy and happiness. Her father was the sun god, Ra. Her head was like a lioness's.

The Ancient Egyptians made statues of cats to honour Bastet. They made their statues out of materials they thought would last forever, like gold and bronze. Year 3 used different things to make their cats but the idea was the same.

Bastet poem

Long after dark our cats sat there
we made them out of papier-mâché
and Pringle cans
salt and vinegar, barbecue flavour,
(some even had the crumbs left in).
But a bastet is a bastet
and their souls will fly no matter
what their bodies are made of.

We helped each other wrap them
in miles and miles of blue bandage,
some white or pink or yellow
But a bastet is a bastet
and their souls will soar no matter
the colour of their wrapping.
We used paint to make their faces,
cat eyes and cat noses
though we forgot the ears and whiskers.
But a bastet is a bastet
and their souls will live no matter
that their faces are not finished.
Through the night
they sat
side by side on the shelf
in the corridor
waiting for the afterlife
and in the morning
we gave them names
to take with them
on their journey
and wrote our names on the bottom
so we could take them home.

Sonnet means 'little song'. Traditionally sonnets have fourteen lines. The last two lines normally rhyme with each other.

William Shakespeare wrote many beautiful love sonnets that have lasted a very long time.

Someone in Year 3 had a good idea about how to make wishes last for ever.

This is a sonnet about that.

Sonnet of wishes

There are as many different ways to make
A single wish as there are falling stars;
Birthday candles lit upon a cake,
Maidens spinning gold inside a tower.
And when the yellow dandelion flower
Dries soft from sunny blonde to lady grey,
One pluck, one breath releases to the air
A fleet of fairy wishes on their way.
But what about the genie in his lamp
Who wakens with a rub and then appears,
Welcoming the very first command,
The one that flies the fastest to his ears.
If such a chance came knocking at your door
Would you not wish to make a thousand more?

What do teachers get up to when we're not watching them?

Where do they go at the end of the school day?

Why are they so good at spelling?

Some of us think we know...

My teacher's a witch

My teacher has great big black shoes
and skinny long legs under a long black skirt
My teacher's a witch
(well she's not really, but I like to pretend she is)
And when she says STOP! she turns everyone into statues
(well we're not really, but I like to pretend we are)
and we're frozen there and we can't do anything
And when she's very cross and fed up
she can put a spell on us to make us good
so we won't annoy her any more.
She has a broomstick, too,
and she lets us use it when it's tidy-up time
but it never works when we try to ride on it.
It works for my teacher, though.

Every day when I see her coming out of school
when I'm going home
from the after-school club
she says to me, 'Hello, Christopher,
must fly!'
and she disappears on her broomstick
(well it's a bicycle really, but I like to pretend it isn't)
And the next morning she's always there at her desk
ready to make new magic for the day.

Some of the children in this school have known each other since they were babies. They went to Nursery together then Reception. They were in the same class in Year 1 and Year 2 and now they're in the Juniors together. Not everyone though. Some children move away and go to a new school somewhere else. Sometimes new children move to this school.

I remember when I was new. Do you?

New kid

There's a new kid coming soon
to our class, to our school
New kid, new kid
It's cos Holly had to go
and she isn't coming back
Said she's moved into a mansion
and her bedroom's painted black,
said she'd write us all a postcard
but we haven't had one yet
I'm not really going to miss her
Cos she was our teacher's pet.

So there's this new kid coming now
to our class, to our school
New kid, new kid
What will they be like?
Will they be weird, will they be cool?
Sandra thinks that they'll be bossy
and try to make new rules
Hanzra thinks they might be ugly
Kieron thinks they will be fat
Bet the teacher's crossing fingers
that it's Holly coming back.

It's today the new kid's coming
to our class, to our school
New kid, new kid
the desk next to me is empty
where Holly used to be
I guess that means the new kid
will be sitting next to me
Noor says she'll probably smell bad
Tom says he won't speak English
Miss tried to stop us guessing
but asked us all what we wished.

This new kid who'll be coming
to our class, to our school
New kid, new kid
Would you like them to be clever
or would you rather they were not?
What if they have a packed lunch
that smells like a curry shop?
Should they wear a baseball cap
or a turban on their head?
Should they say their prayers to Allah
or a different God instead?

Should they go to church on Sundays
or to the synagogue?
Does it matter if their father's rich
or if he doesn't have a job?

What if their face is spotty
or they have a funny nose?
What if their eyes are slanty
or they walk with turned in toes?

She said, imagine you were coming
to our class, to our school
A new kid, new kid
Would you be excited
or would you be a little scared?
Would you be missing all your old friends
and wish that they were there?
What would you do at playtime
if no one lets you in their game?
Being new is different
and nothing feels the same.

The new kid's coming in now
to our class, to our school
New kid, new kid
Everyone's excited
We're all turning round to see
My heart's thumping fast now
cos he's sitting next to me
The teacher stands up quietly
Something's changed in its own way
She says now everyone is new
We're a different class today.

Imagine your life was like a book you could make crossings out and addings to.

There might be some things you'd change but certain things you'd decide to leave exactly as they are.

Friends

Think of all the people you have known
and the ones you haven't met yet
Think of the parties, the sleepovers,
the games, the conversations
Think of the walks and the talks
and all the silly arguments
Think of all the times you've felt happy
and all the times you've felt sad
Think of all the things you'd like to do
and all the things you've done.

If you had it to do all over again
Would I still be your best friend?

At this school they had Circle Time where anyone could talk about anything they wanted to.

I think it's a very good idea and I wish there were Circle Times everywhere, for everyone, even grown-ups.

Circle time

I have this friend, see,
and he's always saying
that at playtime
no one will play with him
and I know it's true
because I've seen him there
standing all alone
wishing he could join in.

I know how it feels
when people say
there's no room
in the game for you.

I know how slowly
the time can go
when everyone else
is playing, but you.

Sometimes I think
I should tell him
I know what it's like
to be all alone
But knowing my friend
it wouldn't make any difference
It would just be a bit
like talking to myself.

Learning about science doesn't always happen in the classroom.

3KB went into the playground in pairs and measured themselves and their shadows in the sun.

Topic work in Science

With pieces of chalk
we drew around our shadows
till we didn't fit

Shadows drawn at noon
grew from babies to giants
by going home time

A poem doesn't have to be capitalised or written in whole sentences like a story does – if you want you can write a whole poem without using a single full stop – that is sometimes the way thinking happens, on and on without stopping – your brain tugs you along so fast you have to ask it to wait – like going for a walk with a friend

Wait for me

wait for me,
i'll go with you
i just need
to tie my shoe
there it's done
now shall we walk
we could have
a little talk
are you free
to come around
ask your mum
i've got a pound
if you want
we'll get some sweets
we could fix
a midnight feast
let's pretend
we've run away
orphan kids
who've lost their way
we could make
a little house
live in it
all by ourselves
you could cook
and i could clean
no one else
would have a key
what if we
were very rich...
wait a sec
i've got an itch
my head hurts
my feet are sore
i can't stay
out any more
there's my dad
i've got to go
he gets cross
if i'm too slow
help me tie
my other shoe
tomorrow
i will wait for you

When I was seven my teacher read the poem 'Stopping by Woods on a Snowy Evening' by Robert Frost, to our class. I loved the sound of it, and the feel of it.

Sometimes a great poem by someone else can inspire you to write a poem of your own. Robert Frost's poem inspired me to write this one.

My corner

I have a corner where I go
A place that no one really knows
It's where I sit to have my thoughts
And plan my life out, I suppose

It's quite a quiet little spot
As quiet goes, it's all I've got
When people ask me where I've been
Don't know if I should tell or not

There are lots of other kids I've seen
(Who need that sort of space, I mean)
But in this place I'm all alone
So I'm not telling anything

Though I don't have a bed or phone
My corner's like a little home
That I'll remember when I've grown
That I'll remember when I've grown

Year 3 couldn't always agree on what game
to play at playtime.

I like to read this one out loud. I usually
take a deep breath before I start and then
I say it all quickly, in one go, getting faster
and faster and louder and louder because
that's the way it happened when I wrote it.

You say

You say let's play Cops and Robbers
but last time we played
I fell over and hurt my leg
and you said I had to go to jail anyway.
OK, you say, Sticky Toffee then
but Miss Lianni said we weren't
to play that any more
because the last time
the person on the end
had their shoelace undone
and tripped everyone else up.

Fine, you say, Space Aliens,
but don't you remember we could never
agree on the rules to that one because
Sophie thinks there should be a safe planet
and you said we can only have
Time Out, not Home. You say, right,
well how about Dodge Ball?
But those girls from Year 4 are already using
the ball for playing Lazy Susan.
OK, you say, Duck, Duck, Goose. But
no one else wants to play that
OK, you say, but you really don't
look OK, you look a bit mad.
OK, you say
What are we going to play?
and, honest, I was just about to say
when the bell rang to say
no more play
Great, you say
Let's go in.

Half term.
   A whole week without any school.
   But when you're back, everyone
wants to know...

What did you do...
on your holiday?

Did you climb the pyramids in Egypt
or see tigers in Nepal?
Did you go skiing in the Alps
or climb the Chinese Wall?
Did you swim alongside dolphins
in the Caribbean Sea?
Or did you stay in watching telly
doing nothing, just like me?

Did you ride camels in the desert
or camp underneath the stars?
Did you go to Monte Carlo
to see the racing cars?
Did you see Niagara fall
or the Pisa Tower lean?
Or did you lie across the sofa
and read a magazine?

Dear Granny
We have been
to the park,
to the shops
and to the
LIBRARY. It's
BRILLIANT
Lots of Love

Did you buy a brand new bicycle
and join the Tour de France?
Did you watch a Spanish bullfight
or a real flamenco dance?
Did you ride a bucking bronco
or the Orient Express?
Or did you stay right where you were
at the same old same address?

Did you go to Disneyland
Jamaica or Peru?
Did you paraglide or bungee jump
do judo or kung fu?
Did you see monkeys in the jungle
or buffalo on the plain?
Or did you have to feed the rabbit
next door, in the rain?

On second thoughts, don't tell me
what you did or where you went.
Don't tell me what you saw
or all the money that you spent.
And please don't think of asking me
or I might have to say
that staying right here close to home
was a perfect holiday.

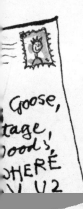

Goose,
tage,
ood's,
HERE
U 2

'Sticks and stones can break my bones
but words can never hurt me...'
  I am not so sure that is always true.
Some words can hurt.
  But the right words can help you to
feel better. The right words and a little
help from friends.

What I do when someone calls me stupid (for George)

What I do when someone calls me stupid...

First of all I know they're wrong,
then I find that place inside where I am strong

I walk away with my head held tall
till I find someone that I can call
a friend
a friend

When I'm feeling bad, like I don't count

I remember what a huge amount

of things there are to do with me
that kids who bully just can't see

Things that they can't take away
no matter what they do or say

These are the things that make me great
(but it still feels hard being only eight!)

And finally when they call me names
and stop me playing in their games

I give myself a hug inside
so I never have to run and hide

I hope to God I'll never be
as mean to them as they are to me

And before their game can reach an end
I turn around and see
a friend
a friend.

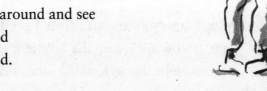

Do you know that rhyme about magpies?

'One for sorrow, Two for joy...'
Some people say that if you see a magpie by itself, you should salute and say 'Good morning Mr. Magpie' or you might have bad luck.

You're not supposed to walk under ladders either, or put your shoes on the table.

But I'm not sure good luck is anything to do with how many magpies you see.

I'm not superstitious

I'm not superstitious but when I wake up in the morning I always stretch one of my arms towards the window and the other towards the door so that I know it will be a good day.

I'm not superstitious but before I get dressed I find my yellow sock with the hole in it and put my finger right through to the other side before I get out clean socks and a vest to wear.

I'm not superstitious but on my way to the kitchen before breakfast I turn around three times and say Coco Pops just to make sure there is some left in the box when I get there.

I'm not superstitious but when my dad asks me if I've remembered to do my homework I cross my fingers and put them behind my back before I say 'Yes!' just in case I really haven't.

I'm not superstitious but I have to remember to put my lucky orange feather in my pocket to bring to school to stop me from crying if someone is mean to me.

I'm not superstitious but if I don't give my mum a big hug and a kiss before I leave the house in the morning she says she won't make it through the day without feeling sad.

I'm not superstitious but my mum is.

This poem is a sestina. Each verse
has six lines and there are six words
(or variations of them) which get
repeated in a different order at the
end of each line. To finish, all six words
get used again in the last three lines.

The rules for writing a poem like
this are complicated, just like life can
be sometimes.

Mumdadmehomeschoolfriends
(sestina)

Ten minutes to nine and already my mum
Has shouted three times from downstairs to tell me
If I don't come soon I will be late for school,
And she's already said that I can't stay home
Because she'll be at work. "So, what about Dad?"
I ask. She ignores me and says, "There's your friend."

The girl from next door is not really a friend.
"If we run, we'll catch up," says my mother,
But she won't be running in those shoes that Dad
Thinks are even too pink and too pointy for me,
Says he won't be seen dead with her outside the house,
But I like how she looks when she takes me to school.

Plenty of people think my mother is cool
And it's nice showing her off to all of my friends,
But they're always asking to play at my house
And she says they're welcome. She's like that, my mum.
But I'd rather have no one invited but me,
I prefer it at home when it's just Mum and Dad.

They're always talking, my mother and father
About whether I'm happy with friends at my school.
Sometimes it feels like they don't even know me,
I've got my telly and five different pen pals.
I never feel lonely, I said to my mum,
I don't want it different at school or at home.

One day I think that I'll walk in the house
And find Mum with somebody else who's not Dad.
Somebody else who'll be calling her Mother.
I think that they've planned it while I've been at school,
Preparing the ground for a new little friend,
Though I'm perfectly happy it just being me.

If I squeeze her hand tight she might know what I'm
Thinking. "You all right?" she says while she's holding
Her arm around me like I'm her best friend.
Says her feet hurt. "Serves her right," waves my dad.
I hope we take ages getting to school,
Just the two of us walking. Me and my mum.

When we get to the school there's no sign of my friends.
In the empty playground Mum skips with me
Across the black tarmac. Dad will laugh later, at home.

Abbreviations are a way of making things shorter, for writing or saying or doing.

In this school there were lots of abbreviations.

Order of the day (abbreviated)

Now then class 3SC, finish up your EMR. It will soon be time for EMW and before break we will need to do our LH at which point it will be straight out for MMP... well, look outside, Keir, you tell me, do we need jackets?... after which we will be doing our usual NH followed by ST... yes, Holly, I know it's your turn... closely succeeded by lunch. I'd like some help from the LTMs... no Jake, I've got you down as a PGH, not a CM... to make sure no lunch boxes get left behind like last time. If all goes well after LTP and I've had no bad reports from the SMSAs we will be joined by class 3KB for DEX and then Miss Wyatt from 5RW will come to talk to us about our Science Projects. Those who know they will be sharing, I'd like you in paired groups of three please. That's JRM with BMK and YHR with TKG.

You all know who you are so let's have no mucking about, no horseplay and definitely no TWP. That's talking without permission for any of you who might have forgotten. OK?

3SC	Ms Chapman's class
EMR	early morning reading
EMW	early morning work
LH	literacy hour
MMP	mid-morning play
NH	numeracy hour
ST	showing time
LTM	lunchtime monitors
PGH	playground helper
CM	class monitor
LTP	lunchtime play
SMSA	dinner lady
3KB	Ms Beach's class
DEX	daily exercises (like they do in New Zealand where Ms Beach is from)
5RW	Ms Wyatt's class in year 5!!!
JRM	James B, Roxanne, Martha
BMK	Begum, Max, Keir
YHR	Yasmin, Henry, Rosa
TKG	Tinuke, Kane, George
TWP	(ibid.)
ibid.	ibidem – Latin word meaning mentioned before

TMA
(Too many abbreviations)

Year 3 had to do a spelling test every week.

Miss Chapman and Miss Beach would decide on the words and put them on a piece of paper for everyone to take home and study.

Not everyone liked having to study for their spelling test. Some people couldn't see why they had to.

Especially when they were words you already knew perfectly well!

Spelling test

Don't
Can't
Couldn't
Won't
Shouldn't
Wouldn't
Doesn't
Needn't (optional)

I **don't** want to do my spellings
Because I **can't** do my spellings
I **couldn't** care less about my spellings
And **won't** want to do them ever
I **shouldn't** have to do my spellings
You **wouldn't** want to either
If everybody **doesn't** do their spellings
Then we really **needn't** bother!

Rules tell you what you can do and can't do.
There are school rules and home rules. There are
rules for playing games. There are even poem rules.
   The rules for writing a villanelle are:

1. You are only allowed two rhyme sounds
   (I chose 'ay' and 'ed').
2. The first line and the third line have to stay
   separate but keep coming back, on their own,
   every five lines, until they are allowed to
   come back together finally at the end.
3. There should be nineteen lines altogether.
   If you write twenty, it's too much.
4. Five of the verses have three lines but the
   last one is allowed four.
5. There is no rule about what the poem
   should be about. I think that's a secret.

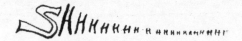

Secrets (villanelle)

The secrets you are not allowed to say
Lie crouching somewhere deep inside your head
Like it's a game of hide and seek they have to play.

Sometimes when you have a friend to stay
And you're both lying there whispering in bed
The secrets you are not allowed to say.

Then you have to snatch it back and pray
That no one will remember what you said
Like it's a game of hide and seek they have to play.

If only they could sleep all night and day
Or live in someone else's head instead
The secrets you are not allowed to say.

I would be happier if things could be that way
What if they live long after you are dead
Like a game of hide and seek they'll always play?

Perhaps if I had wings to fly away
I would not have to live in constant dread
The secrets you are not allowed to say
Might hide, and seek another game to play.

I grew up in America. We used to go on very long car journeys. It took two whole days to drive from where I lived in Colorado to where one of my Grandmas lived in Pennsylvania.

Being in a car for so long is boring.

I rode in the back with my two sisters. We read, argued, played games, argued, sang songs, argued, looked out the window, and argued.

Sometimes I would say things to myself in my head. A word, a sound, anything. To pass the time I might say it again over and over just to see how it sounded.

Rubbish

Rubbish Rubbish Rubbish Rubbish Rubbish Rubbish
Rubbish Rubbish Rubbish Rubbish
Rubbish
Rubbish
Rubbish
Rubbish Rubbish, Rubbish Rubbish
Rubbish, Rubbish, Rubbish
Rubbish, Rubbish, Rubbish, Rubbish, Rubbish, Rubbish,

You know how when you say a word
so many times that it stops making sense?
No... rubbish!!

Invitations are special.

You can send them on nice paper or pretty card, or you can just tell someone they are invited.

You can say something like 'Please come...' or 'It would be a Pleasure to have your Company' or 'We'd be delighted if...' Whenever someone is having a party there will be people who are invited to it. But it is not always you.

The party

Lola's having a big party
but she isn't having me
Everyone's invited
and they're going there at three

Lola says she couldn't ask me
she was only allowed ten
But everybody's going and
I thought I was her friend

Mum said not to worry
we'll do something else instead
But all I feel like doing
is sitting on my bed

I've got this hollow feeling
like there's nothing left inside
Mum said I should try eating
but it doesn't work, I've tried

I could put my woolly hat on
so it covers up my ears
And maybe wear my magic cloak
I haven't worn in years

I could try on Mummy's slippers
or my brother's football socks
I could put on loads of glitter
from my brand new make-up box

I'll get out all the dress-ups
and paint my toenails green
And tie my hair up properly
so I look about sixteen

I'm going to rearrange my room
so it looks a little arty
Then I'll get out all my animals
and we can have a party

I'll blow on all my whistles
and bang my tambourine
I'll play music very loudly
on my sister's tape machine

Mum will ask what all the noise is,
can she come up and see?
I'll say, "Yes, you are invited,
we will be starting around three!"

When you've had a fight with someone
it's hard to stop thinking about it.

Some people say you should never let
the sun set on an argument.

It would be better if everyone said sorry
straight away, but it doesn't always
work out like that.

Don't let the sun go down

These are difficult days,
even the squirrels
and the birds outside my window
don't seem to be able to get along.

Last night I went to sleep
before anyone said sorry.
And I thought the sun was
never supposed to go down
on an argument,
I thought no one would ever let me
sulk past my bedtime.

My dreams were full of hairy, scary things,
wild eyes and loud, shouty voices.

There were no stairways to heaven,
no scoring of championship points
or kisses from princes
in the stories I dreamt.

This morning the sun came up
as usual.
And I knew the night had hoovered up
some of the fighting,
lighting it up like little stars,
twinkling reminders of things that are
truly important.

I know I can't stop the birds twittering,
the squirrels chattering,
the bickering
or the battering
but I can sing a song, loudly,
on my way down to breakfast.

Finding a penny that someone else has
dropped is supposed to bring good luck.
   But what about all the people that
don't find one?

Find a penny

Find a penny pick it up
all your life you'll have good luck

Throw it back upon the ground
spread all that good luck around

Bad feelings can stay like a lump in your
throat or a heavy weight in your belly.
But not forever, hopefully.

Grudges

I thought grudges went away
but apparently they don't
they grow and grow
like potato tubers
until there are so many tendrils
so many roots
so many hard, hard
nuggets of grief
that no matter how hard you try
even if you clear the ground completely
one or two will be left there
to spread out
and grow again.

Maybe the only thing to do
is to leave the grudge
where it is
buried deep
to wait patiently while it spreads itself
and grows
multiplying a thousand times over
to wait and to watch
until one tiny part of it
finally emerges
breaking through hard mud
packed ground
reaching upwards
towards the light
budding into flower.

It doesn't always show when something hurts. Aches and pains can be invisible.

The problem with invisible things is that some people don't believe they're real.

Headache

It's a fuzzy kind of fuzziness,
this thud inside my head.
It was thudding there this morning
and the night before in bed.

I thought headaches were for grown-ups,
like credit cards and loans.
I didn't think a kid like me
should have to moan and groan.

It's hard to watch the whiteboard,
when I close my eyes it's worse.
I'll put my hand across my forehead
and pretend that I'm a nurse.

My mum thinks that I'm faking it,
she made me come to school.
Unless you've got a temperature...
she says. (Her golden rule!)

Why won't they believe you
when you say that something hurts?
It's impossible to prove it
if they don't feel it first.

There's something about these grown-ups,
my teacher's just the same.
They think that our complaining
is part of some big game.

If they could just remember
when they were only nine,
and someone bigger told them,
You're not ill, you seem just fine.

I don't mean to be dramatic,
honestly I don't.
But I'm going to start to howl now
and gurgle in my throat.

I'm going to double over
and clutch my stomach hard.
I'll writhe around in pain
and wave my kidney donor card.

I'm going to fall on to the floor
and play like I am dead.
It's the only way they'll understand
this ache inside my head.

When you haven't done something
you were supposed to do, it's a
good idea to explain why.

But the teacher won't always
believe you.

Excuses

Sir, my pencil sharpener's broken
Sir, and that's not all
Sir, my bag got torn to pieces
when I was climbing on the wall

Sir, I didn't do my spellings cos
Sir, there was no time
Sir, my auntie's here from China
she's one hundred and ninety-nine

Sir, I have to leave school early
Sir, I'll bring a note in from my mum
Sir, my brother's gone to hospital
he's bitten off his thumb

Sir, I can't go out at playtime
Sir, there's a blister on my toe
Sir, my trousers are too small for me
I need to wait for them to grow

Sir, I never got the homework
Sir, it wasn't in my drawer
Sir, my grandpa has no hearing
it was damaged in the war

Sir, I wasn't interrupting
Sir, I am trying to be good
Sir, I promise I'll do everything
you told me that I should

Sir, I'm not making up excuses,
Sir, there'd be no excuse for that
Sir, I excuse you for accusing me
I'm so glad we had this chat.

There are all kinds of ways of taking the morning register.

At this school the teacher made it sound like the children were grown-ups.

When we're all grown-up

When all the girls are ladies
and the boys have turned to men
Everything will be completely
different, then
We'll all be driving motor cars,
and learning how to kiss
And taking morning register
would sound like this:

>Good morning Mr Bhutta,
>and to you Ms Goldenberg,
>Good morning dear Ms Imran,
>you're moving house, I've heard.
>Good morning there, Ms Braemar
>and good day to you Ms Scott,
>Welcome back Ms Austin,
>you've been on holiday have you not?
>Good morning Mr Charalambou,
>Good morning Mr Skewes,
>Ms Mann, I have to ask you,
>where did you get your shoes?
>How are you Ms Freeman,
>very well I hope,

Ms Morton, Mr Houghton,
is it true that you've eloped?
Hello Mr Battcock,
Mr Gillian, Mr Kee,
Good morning Mr Lacey,
is that bunch of flowers for me?
Good morning Mr Cavalier
and Ms McAtominey,
Ms Gavin, I hardly knew you,
you've changed your hair I see.
Good morning Mr Kemplan,
Good morning Mr Fitzke,
Mr Fevre, I do believe
you smell a bit of whisky!

Good morning Mr Cunliffe
and to you Ms Galvin, dear,
Ms de Miguel, it's such a pleasure
to have your presence here.
Mr Malinowski,
how nice to see you sir,
Good morning Ms O'Yediran,
(sniff) is that Eau de Fleur?
Mr Matthews, if I may,
you're looking very smart,
Ms Scipio, good morning,
that suit's a work of art!

When all the girls are ladies
and the boys have become men
We wouldn't write in pencil,
we'd get to use a pen.
We'd put on clothes like suits and ties
and high heels I expect
And our teacher (who'd be ancient)
would treat us with great respect!

I like the rain but it can make people grumpy if it goes on too long. Everyone has to stay indoors and think of things to do until it's dry enough to go out.

Wet play

It's wet play
  today
    No way
      are we going outside

        where it's raining dogs and cats
        at least that's
        what Mr Wilson said
        I think it is more
          like splats
          a giant cow has made

The playground's wet
  and can't be dried
    the window's misted up
      inside
        and someone's drawn a smiley face
        at least
          they've tried

Miss is getting cranky
  says she really
    hates the rain
        She keeps telling off Muhammed
        Says he's being
          a constant pain
            Serena's got the chalk
              and says she's thought of
              a new game

She's put Hangman on the board
  and the word
    we have to guess
      has three letters in it
      and one of them
          is 'S'
            But we don't know the others
            and now we're really
            in a mess

We've tried 'B' and 'V' and 'W'
    and 'X' and 'Y' and 'Z'
      And Serena's drawn two legs
        two arms
          a body
            and a head
              Lucy starts to cry
                because
                  the hanged man
                  will be dead

Miss tells Lucy
  not to snivel
    She says Hangman should be fun
      And then we look outside
        and see that now
          the raining's done
            And suddenly
              I know the word
                I say, Serena
                  Is it S-u-n ?

We all have favourite words. Maybe we like them because of the way they look when they're written down.

Or because of what they mean.

Or maybe we don't even know what they mean but we like the way they sound when you say them.

Some words sound especially good.

Onomatopoeia rap

Listen while I tell you 'bout a word that really rocks
It jiggles like a jelly and it pongs like smelly socks
It wraps itself around you like an anaconda squeeze
And sets your teeth a chattering while you shiver
    and you freeze
It crashes and it bangs and it really makes a clatter
It can fill you till you pop, or squash you till you're flatter
It bubbles when it boils and it sizzles when it fries
It glitters and it dazzles and it really takes the prize
If you want a word that matters, and lingers in your ear
Try an onomato onomato onomatopoeia!

3SC had a class pet.

Everyone looked after him during term time.

On holidays and at the weekends the children took it in turns to take him home.

When he died they made a book about him and put his name and picture on the front.

Our class hamster

Our class hamster was an onomatopoeia.
We called him
Cuddles.

There are lots of ways to go to other places.
    You can go by boat, on a plane, or through your imagination.

Elephant at my window

There's an elephant disguised as a tree outside my window
It bends and waves its long trunk so enthusiastically
there must be a whole herd of them coming in my direction
It is a long way from Africa
here in my bedroom
where grey light plays games with the sun
and dances like a safari
wild jungle on my wall.

Kids are good at clapping games.
Grown-ups aren't.
I think that's the main difference.

Clapping games for two

Do you know...

Under the bramble bush
down by the sea
boom boom boom
true love for you my darling
true love for me
and when we marry...

I'm not

What?

Going to marry.

Why not?

Yuck!!

That's not very nice to the person
    you're going to marry.

I'm not

What?

Going to marry.

Why not?

Yuck!!

That's not very nice to the person
    you're going to marry.

I'm not

What?

Going to marry...

Yeah, I know.

Harry is a genius

Harry is a genius
That's what my mummy said
He's got alphabets and numbers
Whizzing round his head

His brain is a computer
Like my Pentium PC
It must be all the microchips
That Harry has for tea

If Harry really likes you
He'll tell you all he knows
Why most owls only hoot at night
And where the north wind blows

He'll show you how a compass works
And where Guam is on the map
He's never bored or tired
Mum says geniuses don't nap

Harry is a genius
He does algebra for fun
He can calculate the distance
From his house to the sun

His socks are different colours
And his shoes are never tied
He writes his name with his left hand
I use the other side

He can spell words like Larynx
Thyroid and Thesaurus
He knows which one is bigger
T. Rex or Brontosaurus

When our teacher asks for quiet
Harry keeps on talking
He taps his feet and moves about
Our teacher calls it 'rocking'

Harry is a genius
And he's coming round for tea
Mum thinks Harry's greatest genius
Is being friends with me!

Some words make you think about
what matters a lot, and what
doesn't so much.

Like big, bigger, biggest.
Or good, better...

Best

Best friend for always
but in-between
sometimes not.

Best in class at Maths
apart from Jenny
she's quite good.

Best thing in lunch box
chocolate digestives
foil wrapped.

Not everything from when you're young
will stay in your memory.

Writing poems is a good way of
remembering the things you want to.

I wonder what you'll remember when
you're a grown-up.

Some things I will remember

There are things I will remember
when I'm older
that I can't remember now

the feel of my mother's hand
on my back when I can't sleep

the smell of the Junior Hall
on Thursdays when they have
chips and spaghetti rings
for school dinners

the smell of my lunch box
when Dad's made me tuna fish
sandwiches

the way grown-ups' eyes puff up
the same whether they've been
asleep or crying

the butterflies I get when someone
says something funny
and only a few people understand
and I'm one of them.

The faces of everyone I love.

Finally it's the end of the day, and there's nothing more that needs to be said or done except...

I love you... more

You know what?
What?
I love you
I love you more
Impossible
It's not
I'm afraid it is, now go to sleep
OK. I love you
I love you more
No you don't, it's not possible
Yes it is, now, quiet
Mum?
I'm putting the light out. What?
Do you love me?
Yes, spades, now shhh...
Well I love you buckets
I love you gallons
I love you bushels
Well I love you truckfuls

I love you trainfuls
I love you acres
I love you miles
Well I love you tons
I love you hundredweights
I love you thousands
I love you millions
I love you billions
I love you trillions
I love you quadrillions
I love you zillions
Well I love you zillions and zillions
I love you googolplex

What's that?
Everything. Infinity and beyond... and besides
you can't say any more
Why?
Because I love you more than you can say
any day, any way hooray
and everything I say is possible
OK?

OK.
Good night.

Cheryl Moskowitz writes poetry, plays and
fiction for adults and children. She works
regularly as a writer and storyteller in schools.
Her play *Granny's Bottom Drawer* was the first
production specifically for under-5s
to be commissioned by Quicksilver Theatre
for Children, for whom she also wrote
No. 3 Pied Piper Street. Her poetry for children
has featured on BBC TV's A Bear Behind
and CBeebies' Poetry Pie series. Her novel
Wyoming Trail was published by Granta
in 1997, and *The Girl Is Smiling*, her poetry
collection for adults, was published by
Circle Time Press in 2012.
She lives in London, is married to a musician
and has three children.

MORE POETRY FROM
FRANCES LINCOLN CHILDREN'S BOOKS

978-1-84780-341-2 • PB • £5.99

Meet sensational scorers, dependable defenders,
great goalkeepers and fanatical fans like Great Gran.
Find out who always shouts at the ref,
what is scary about being in the wall and
why you shouldn't put Mum in goal.
Every aspect of the football season and more
are brilliantly brought to life by poet
and football fan Paul Cookson, Poet-in-Residence
at the National Football Museum.

'Dazzling football poetry.' BBC Sport

978-1-84780-166-1 • PB • £5.99

An A-Z of animal poems with a difference!
Choose your favourite from Roger McGough's
witty and wicked menagerie.

"Classic Roger McGough" – *Guardian*

Poems and Drawings by
R●GER McGOUGH

978-1-84780-321-4 • PB • £5.99

This brilliant collection is full of wit,
wordplay and wisdom from Roger McGough...

"A word juggler who never misses a catch"
Charles Causley

978-1-84780-269-9 • PB • £5.99

Funny, fantastic, outrageous, wise...
a powerful mix of comic and serious verse
from one of the UK's most popular poets.

"wild and witty" – *Telegraph*

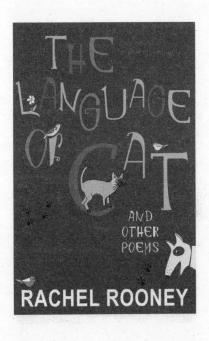

978-1-84780-167-8 • PB • £5.99

With wordplay and riddles, and poems that will make you laugh, tell you stories and make you think, this is a brilliant debut from an exciting new poet.

"A box of delights" – *Carol Ann Duffy*

Poems by
TONY MITTON

978-1-84780-169-2 • PB • £5.99

From spooky legends to dreamy poems, teasers
and rhymes, expect the unexpected. A poetry adventure
waiting to happen!

**"A poet with a powerful feeling for story
and language"** – *Carousel*

978-1-84780-168-5 • PB • £5.99

Perfect for younger children, these poems are fresh,
funny and brilliant for reading aloud.

"These poems are born out of years of visiting
infant classrooms. A real birthday party of words" –
Pie Corbett